Tainted

A Lost Innocence

As a team we travelled to 13 countries, experienced numerous instances of sorrow and poverty, and met countless people who were living trapped in terrible situations. Of all the people we encountered, the faces and lives of children spoke the loudest. We realized that these children were helpless, neglected, and in need of love. Generations in the past had made choices leading to this place of suffering and entrapment. These children had never chosen these tainted circumstances and had no power to change them.

Many children live at the center of injustice, their innocence stolen, helpless to fight back or even cry out. They have no perception of a better life and have never been given the chance to dream or to hope. We realized children need love, but through our travels came to understand they need more then that.

They need action to be sprung from a pure and deep love that knows no bounds. From that place, the cycle can be broken and they can finally be given a chance to break free from oppression.

Can our choices, filled with love, speak louder than the choices of generations past? Can our choices change the lives of these children, bring them hope, and break the cycle of destruction?

*Children are the hope
for tomorrow and
our responsibility for
today.*

We have no safety, no way to protect
ourselves.
We sit on street corners yearning for
more than coins in a tin.
We hide behind thin sheets and small
boards, sleeping on cold, hard misery.

We're the ones with a helpless plea
and a desperate cry behind our
smiling eyes.
We're the ones who never chose to be
here or to live this way.
We're the ones who know that
tomorrow will be the same as today.

We are the children.
We are the future.
And yet we have no hope, no dreams.
We have never perceived the
possibility for more.

I look at my sisters.

Then look to the floor.

Cold, hard, unforgiving concrete.

Eighty square meters of misery.

I look at my mother.

Then to the pile that consists of her

entire existence.

Garbage and mismatched

belongings.

She's never hoped for more.

I remember laying on that same

concrete.

I remember sensing a life waiting

for me, far away.

It felt like something that would

never happen to me.

Nothing gave me the hope to dream.

I remember the fear that came

with darkness.

I remember feeling bare.

Every loud noise a startling

reminder that I wasn't safe.

Waiting for the moment rough

hands would find my sleeping body.

I remember the night he grabbed

me.

I remember feeling dirty and

ashamed.

It never washed off.

It never left me.

I remember our hands joined in

marriage.

I remember the same hands formed

into fists.

Twelve years old.

Four years together.

I look at my sisters.
Hear of the hands that lash out at
night.
See the fear in their eyes.
I know that soon the worst will
happen.

The people that saved me gave me
space to hope and dream.
They gave me life and stole me
back from death.
I want the same for my sisters.
I want to take them far away.

Born and raised in a squatters camp next to a Hindu temple in Delhi, India, most of Babli's life has been full of fear. According to some sources, Delhi has the highest rape rate in India,[1] so Babli and her sisters lived each night wondering if they would be safe. Every afternoon, Babli would decorate hands with henna for the small price of five rupees, equivalent to about ten American cents. The money always went to fund her father's alcoholism, until he left the family to fend for themselves. Girls living in the slum are usually married by the age of fourteen or fifteen, with their own children soon to follow. Without a reliable income, they aren't able to provide for their children and the vicious cycle of poverty and desperation continues.

Three years ago, Babli was rescued from the horrible situation she was trapped in. She had the opportunity to learn to read and write Hindi, practice English, and complete vocational training. The education she received has enabled her to work in a steady job. She is working to save up enough money to buy a house and rescue her sisters out of the slum. She dreams of giving her family the same opportunities she received and breaking the cycle of poverty for good.

The horrors of the slum are shocking. Over 50,000 street children live in Delhi alone, over half of whom are illiterate. Since they have no physical address, they are unable to attend public school and consequently are uneducated. On average, they earn 72 rupees each day from begging on the street, just over one American dollar.[2] The children of the slums are exposed to things we could never imagine. Alcoholism runs rampant, funded by the money earned from their begging. Everything is done in the open for all to see and from an early age they are caught up in this lifestyle.

Every 15 seconds, one child under the age of 5 dies in India.

This adds up to nearly two million every year, the largest number in the world.[3]

Catalyst has rescued a number of girls from slums all over Delhi, India. Each of these young women had a life similar to Babli's, but upon entering Catalyst's program, have had their destiny redefined. By the time they graduate, they will have acquired education, safe housing, and a steady job.

www.catalystindia.org

Though Catalyst has been able to rescue many children from the slum, thousands are still living and dying there. Treasure House focuses on working with the ones still suffering in the slums. The center acts as a daycare, keeping the kids off the dangerous streets while providing the basic necessities they cannot even access. They are fed lunch, because it could be the only meal they eat that day. They are given new clothing, because their parents only provide the ratty clothes that portray desperation, bringing them more money when they beg. They are provided with proper hygiene, because it can prevent the most basic fatal illnesses found so often in the slums. They are educated, because future employment could free them from their disadvantaged living situations. One center is currently in operation, but they have started construction on a second building in another part of the city.

Catalyst and Treasure House work closely together and are giving the slum children of Delhi room to fully live and dream again.

www.ywamfmdelhi.com

Some nights I get flash backs. I leave my little home and am back. Back on the streets in clothes tight and plunging. Back to the cat calls and whistles. Back to a place that always repulsed me; yet kept me alive. I was always faithful to the same street, coming back every night and waiting. Waiting for the moment that would put coins in my pocket and death in my chest. The beginning was the hardest. Now it's a rhythm.

Wake up.

Dress myself.

Paint on a mask.

Walk.

Stand.

Wait.

Wait.

Wait.

Then he'll come. Walking slowly, sometimes hesitant, sometimes completely sure of himself. I put on the charm, become someone I'm not. Someone I hope I'll never be again. He'll take my hand and lead me somewhere. It only lasts a short while.

Tonight I look at Jacob and can't believe he's mine. I can't believe he's sleeping safely beside me. The day he was born I was too sick to hold him in my arms, too lost to even desire it. He was an alien to me, conceived by a nameless, faceless man among hundreds. His small face, paler than mine was going to bring me destruction and pain. I would have brought Jacob back to my street with me. The men would have liked that. I would have had more money in my pocket at the end of the night. The people that rescued me didn't let me. I choke down sobs as I think what could have become of him.

What could have become of me.

I hold him close.

Hear his heartbeat. I don't know how much longer this disease will have a hold on my body until I breath my last, but I know he will make it.

He's alive and healthy, and they'll give him a future better than I ever could have hoped for.

I sing him a love song as he sleeps. I love him more than anything. It's a love he's always deserved, and I can finally give it to him.

I can give it to him for as long as I live.

Even before Jacob was born, all the odds seemed to be against him. In the eyes of every Buddhist Thai, his mixed blood gave him automatic bad karma. His HIV-positive mother had no desire to care for him, even if she had been physically able. The son of a prostitute, he seemed destined to make his living by following in his mother's footsteps and selling himself. Thailand is a major destination for pedophiles around the world.

Fortunately, his mother was rescued just before she gave birth. She was moved across the country and cared for by a team of medical professionals. Special precautions were taken to ensure that Jacob did not contract the disease and he now lives a happy, healthy life.

Others have not been so fortunate. There are an estimated 34 million people living with HIV/AIDS worldwide and 10 percent of these are children.[4] In most countries, medical help is readily available, but many hesitate to receive it due to the stigmas attached to the illness.

Home of the Open Heart in Northern Thailand assists HIV-affected women and children like Mahlee and Jacob. They provide a range of services for individuals affected by the disease, including education, orphan care, and hospice care. When children lose their parents to HIV, Home of the Open Heart is eager to welcome them into their family. They desire to see each child supported by a team of five sponsors, each contributing forty dollars every month. The funds provide food, clothing, education, and other necessary expenses. Such a small amount of money can make an enormous difference in the life of one child.

www.homeoftheopenheart.org

I'm holding a gun the length of my body, slowly moving through tall grasses. My target is a small hut. As I step closer and closer I have a decision to make. A decision that will either spare the life of the one I love in the hut or spare my own. Both of us living is not an option; they made that clear. With each step my heart quickens more and more. Soon my heart is a loud drum beating in my ears and my head feels faint. I reach the flap of fabric and push it aside, revealing her holding my cousin. In a voice not my own I tell her to stand up and face me.

Silent tears slide down her cheeks as she looks me straight in the eyes. As the crack of gunpowder rings through the air, the bullet fires straight and true, taking her life and a big part of my own.

I awake with a gasp. Her eyes still staring deeply into mine, the screams still ringing in my ears; chasing my fleeing figure. Sweat is pouring down my face and I wipe it away as I look around. I'm not in a small hut with my commander anymore. I'm in a new place, with new people. I go to school and live a normal life. I no longer kill and destroy but love and desire better things. I declare these things aloud, convincing myself yet again that I'm not a killer anymore.

Even so, I will never forget the countless eyes that looked at me in terror or the screams of desperation. I will never completely wash the blood from my hands or the death from my heart.

Part of myself died in those two years.

I still look for the gentle, 9 year old boy they stole.

I know I will never fully find him.

Only a broken
shell is left.

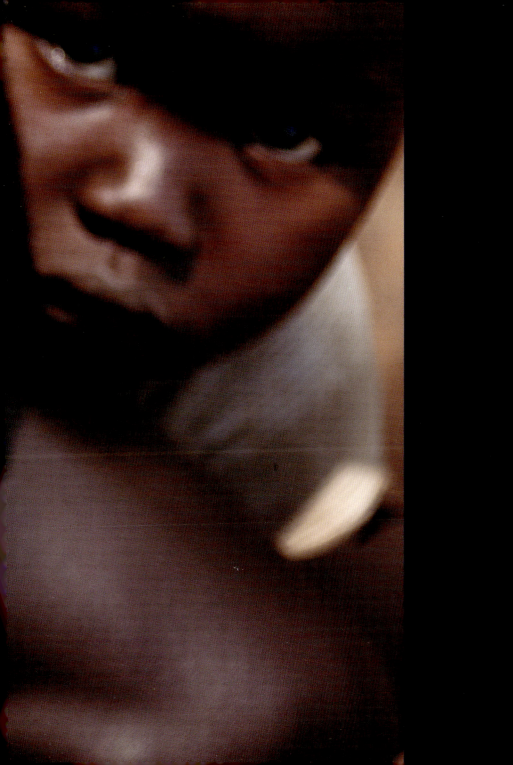

Before the war he was called Thuly, but that name has been brainwashed out of his mind. Samuel is now the only name he knows. Abducted by the Lord's Resistance Army (LRA), a rebel group from Uganda, the nine-year-old boy was easily impressionable. The group indoctrinated him to believe that they did what was best for him and truly loved him. Then they forced him to murder hundreds, including family members, or risk being killed himself. By the time he was rescued two years later, he required an immeasurable amount of rehabilitation in order to integrate back into society.

Joseph Kony, the leader of this rebel group, grew up in a village only fifteen minutes away from Samuel's home.[5]

The group has been abducting children and forcing them to become soldiers for their army since 1987. One in three families in Uganda have lost children to the rebels. Though their activity in Uganda has greatly diminished since 2007, the army has moved into other areas of Central Africa. They continue to terrorize communities and abduct children. Seventy thousand people in South Sudan have been displaced from their homes.[6]

Samuel's family still lives in Northern Uganda, but has begun serving areas of South Sudan affected by the LRA. His uncle has started construction on a building in Issore, South Sudan. Through this building, Issore will be provided with education for the children, agricultural development for the community, and medical care for the sick. The village has begun rebuilding through the help and encouragement of YWAM Arua. Soon they will be able to leave behind the damage caused by the LRAt and begin a new life.

www.ywamarua.wordpress.com

Sometimes I forget.
Sometimes I feel normal, like I have a place I belong and someone I belong to. In that place my belly gets filled and I'm never left with a burning hunger. At night my head hits a warm pillow and I can hear constant, steady breathing. There are people here who watch over me. I know they are close, ready to protect me, comfort me, and love me.

I love Wednesdays.
One day of the week my plate piles high with food and the churchyard fills up with two hundred other children. We play and laugh and I always have arms ready to swing me around and hug me. When I'm there laughter bubbles unchecked from my mouth and I feel like I'm floating on a cloud.

Suddenly I remember.
Suddenly there are mean hands clasped around my arm, leading me away from

safety. It's never the same place he takes me to, but the same thing always happens. I sleep in the corner on the cold hard floor. Instead of hearing steady breathing I hear gasps and groans. I cover my ears and clasp my eyes tightly shut, I know what I'll see when I look over. Every night it's a new lady and I've stopped hoping and waiting for comfort from her. All I've ever received are disgusted looks.

Sometimes I see red.
Sometimes I hit and scream and cry. I feel like I'm going to explode and like there's a big pressure building in my chest.

I hate this.
I hate this man they say is my dad. I hate going from one place to another, never having a home. I hate that I don't belong anywhere. I don't belong to anyone.

Hleleko is one of the innumerable abused children in the world. The emotional state of this beautiful little girl has been destroyed by mistreatment from her parents. Abandoned by her mother, neglected by her father, and exposed to sexual promiscuity at her young age, she knows nothing of normalcy or consistency. Her home situation tells her that she is worth nothing, that no one wants her.

Her father leaves her with a family
in a nearby community whenever
he grows tired of her. The stable
environment in her second home is
conducive to her emotional health.
The longer she lives there, the happier
she gets. However, it seems that each
time she begins to stabilize, her father
takes her away once more and the
cycle begins again.

Abuse affects countless children every year. It is almost impossible to track the global number of children who are harmed by abuse each year, as many cases are never reported. According to a recent survey, however, 25-50% of children world-wide have been physically abused.[7]

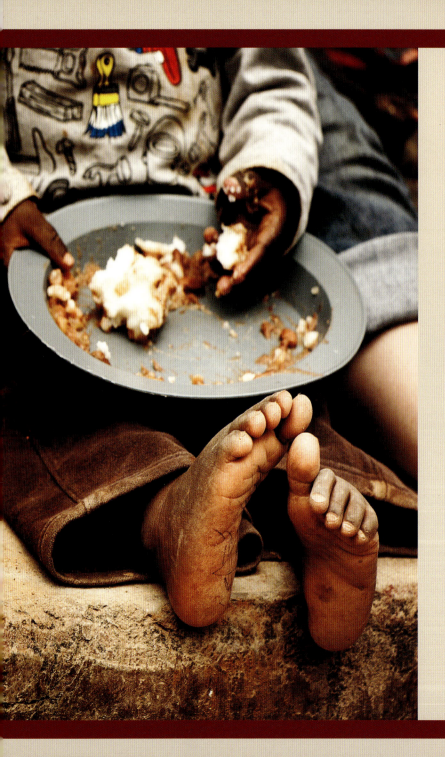

Ten Thousand Homes provides meals, education, and homes for South Africa's vulnerable and orphaned children. Their feeding program serves over five hundred children every week. A donation of only five dollars can feed one of these children for an entire month and enable the staff at Ten Thousand Homes to give love and restore dignity to each of these little ones.

www.tenthousandhomes.org

I step in from the cold sleet coming down in sheets.
I wait inside the door.
I can breathe again; he's not here.
The air feels icy and cool and the small square room of a house smells like mold and mildew.
The paint is peeling, the walls are slightly bent in, about to give up.
I take the small pile of coins out of my pocket and place it on the table. They weren't very generous today.
When he finally comes home I stop breathing.
It's almost as if I stop living.
My walls come up and I get ready for the hands to reach for me.
I peel my damp shirt from my body and close my eyes.
Tonight there's more than one deep voice that greets me.

Tonight there are unfamiliar hands caressing my skin.

From there my mind goes blank.

They talk about sending me to Greece. About me making more money in that distant place.

I close my eyes and breath deeply. I've heard rumors of the work I would have to do there. I don't want it. I have nowhere else to go, no one else I can be.

Sometimes I dream at night. Of a house full of laughter, and people that truly love me. But then I awake, staring at the same roof. With the same brother beside me and the same mother far away.

I'll keep playing this part. I don't know where else to go. I don't know who else to be.

At thirteen years old, Delilah should know nothing of the things she has experienced. When she was only eight years of age, her mother abandoned her and left her with her older brother. Each day, he forced her to beg for money, which he used to finance his alcohol addiction. When he had enough to drink, he would sexually abuse her and invite his friends to do the same. As a result, Delilah began to act up in school and become uncontrollable. Her family thought she was too much to handle and has decided to marry her off to a 21-year-old man who has already been married multiple times. His family is well known for trafficking girls into brothels in the neighboring Greece. She lives with her fiancé now and is highly at risk of becoming a victim of prostitution. Once more, she would be abused by strangers.

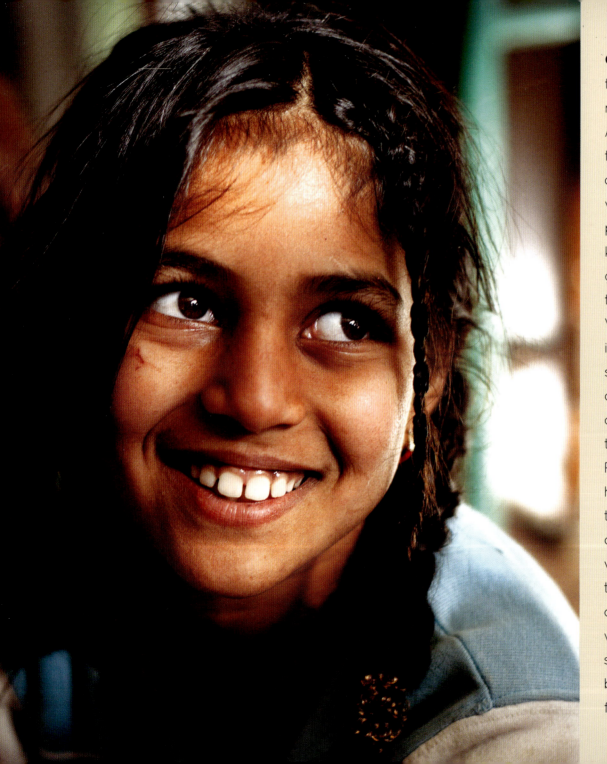

Of the 2.5 million people trafficked every year, nearly half are children.[8] Approximately forty thousand of those are sent to Greece, which has legalized prostitution and is now known as the trafficking gateway to the rest of the European Union.[9] Victims can be forced into anything from sexual exploitation to cheap labor. Delilah could become one of these statistics. Her Roma gypsy community has almost accepted that trafficking is a way of life. She is stuck, without any other place to call home. Soon, her destructive lifestyle will spiral into a worse situation. She needs to be rescued. She must be freed.

The Nest in Pogradec, Albania has been working to do just that. Focusing predominantly on Roma gypsies, they provide basic needs, temporary housing, and education for the disadvantaged children of the neighborhood. Because they are so involved in the community, they are able to keep an eye on children vulnerable to harmful situations, diminishing the frequency of trafficking from that area. However, because the idea has been so ingrained into the mindset of these people, the abolition of this custom has proved to be a difficult task. The Nest will continue to fight against the atrocities happening to each of these little ones and the redemption of just one child is reason enough to celebrate.

www.thenestalbania.com

Children. They are the hope for tomorrow and our responsibility for today. The children we met who inhabit the pages of this book have completely changed our lives and our perspectives. Every one of them is caught up in a tainted lifestyle they cannot control, originating from the consequences of generations past. Their smiling faces mask the difficulty running deep in their bloodlines and the brokenness that consumes their lives. Soon their current situations will affect their choices in the future, either negatively or positively.

We witnessed the power of deep love this year and the change it brought about in the lives of countless children. The love they were shown gave them hope and a new future. It gave them what they needed to make positive choices in their lives, breaking the cycle they were trapped in. Yet there are others who are still in the same place, with the same struggles and the same hopeless, dark outlook. They have never been given the chance to dream and are caught up in lives of poverty and oppression.

One person can make all the difference. *One choice* to help a single child or organization will bring the change we want to see. We have the power and the responsibility to nurture the next generation and *to break the cycle of injustice* in the lives of children all around the world.

It is possible. It is within reach. It is our future.

Dedicated to the many children who touched our hearts and whose stories are left untold.

In memory of
Naomi
New Delhi, India
Unknown-2013

Ad•ven•ture: [ad-ven-cher]

noun

An exciting or very unusual experience.

A bold, usually risky undertaking; hazardous action of uncertain outcome.

And adventure we did. Thank you to everyone that was there for us during these exciting and uncertain 16 months. Thanks be to Jesus, our coordinator and rock, who stood beside us and before us during our entire journey. Paul and Susi, thank you for pioneering PhotogenX and the track program. We are so grateful to be a part of your vision. Layne and Anne, this time would not have been possible without you. Your hard work, dedication, and love for us has been amazing and the memories we have together are priceless. Thank you Fred for blessing our team in India, Argentina, and from Texas. You are an amazing man of God. Joseph Avakian, there would be no book if not for you! You pushed us to be our best and supported us the whole way through, we can never put into words how grateful we are for you. Thank you to Andrew Kooman for your editorial assistance. Thank you to every person and family that showed us amazing hospitality this year. You fed us, housed us, and showed us what real love looks like. Thank you to our teachers who endured harsh conditions, intense humidity, and crazy transportation. We will never be the same because of you. Finally, to our family, friends and supporters: this book, our memories, and our journey were all brought to life by you. You stood by us through it all and we love you so much!

Thank you.

Meet · the · team

Stephnie
Botha
South Africa

Katie
Abrahamson
Canada

Jillian
Bakke
USA

Kelsey
Mcmurry
USA

Sarah
Haberly
USA

Hannah
Cordero
USA

Marielle
Saayman
Canada

Alyssa
Skinner
USA

Kyle
Jaster
Canada

Credits:

Hannah **C**ordero • Photo Editing

Marielle **S**aayman • Writing
Jillian **B**akke • Writing

Alyssa **S**kinner • Design
Katie **A**brahamson • Design

Kyle **J**aster • Production
Sarah **H**aberly • Production
Kelsey **M**cmurry • Production
Stephnie **B**otha • Production

Photos:
Cover: SH
Prologue: KJ
Babli:1. MS 2.MS 3.HC 4.KJ 5.MS 6.KJ 7.MS 8.MS 9.KJ 10.JB
Mahlee & Jacob: 1.AS 2.KJ 3.KJ 4.MS 5.AS 6SH 7.KA
Samuel: 1.KJ 2.SH 3.SH 4.MS 5.KJ 6.MS 7.AS
Hleleko: 1.HC 2.HC 3.JB 4.KJ 5.KJ 6.AS 7.JB
Delilah: 1.KJ 2.KJ 3.KJ 4.KJ 5.JB 6.KJ 7.MS 8KJ
Portraits L-R: 1.SB 2.SB 3.HC 4.KM 5.MS 6.MS 7.JB 8.AS 9.KJ 10.AS 11.KA 12.MS
(Pg.2)L-R:1.KA 2.JB 3.MS 4.HC 5.KJ 6.MS 7.KM 8.AS 9.MS 10.KJ 11.JB 12.KJ 13.MS
14.KM 15.SB 16.MS 17.HC 18.MS 19.HC 20.MS 21.KJ
Thank you: HC
Meet the team: Samantha Aantjes
UofN credit: MS

Printed in China by onthemark. www.onthemark.net

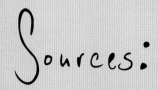

Sources:

1. Mohan, Vishwa. "Delhi remains rape capital." Times of India, October 10, 2011. http://articles.timesofindia.indiatimes.com/2011-10-28/delhi/30332107_1_crime-rate-violent-crimes-crime-incidents (accessed May 16, 2013).
2. Bhaskaran, Dr. Reshmi, and Dr. Balwant Mehta. Save the Children, "Surviving the Streets." Accessed May 16, 2013. http://www.savethechildren.in/images/resources_documents/delhi street children study_v3.pdf.
3. Chamberlain, Gethin. "Two million slum children die every year as India booms." Guardian, October 03, 2009. http://m.guardian-news.com/world/2009/oct/04/india-slums-children-death-rate (accessed May 16, 2013).
4. Avert, "Worldwide HIV & AIDS Statistics." Accessed May 16, 2013. http://www.avert.org/worldstats.htm.
5. "Joseph Kony: Profile of the LRA Leader." BBC, March 08, 2012. http://www.bbc.co.uk/news/world-africa-17299084 (accessed May 16, 2013).
6. The Resolve, "Key Statistics." Accessed May 16, 2013. http://www.theresolve.org/key-statistics.
7. WHO, "Child Maltreatment." Last modified August 2010. Accessed May 16, 2013. http://www.who.int/mediacentre/factsheets/fs150/en/index.html.
8. United Nations, "Human Trafficking: The Facts." Accessed May 16, 2013. http://www.unglobalcompact.org/docs/issues_doc/labour/Forced_labour/HUMAN_TRAFFICKING_-_THE_FACTS_-_final.pdf.
9tt. Ecpat, "Stop Sex Trafficking of Children and Young People." Accessed May 16, 2013. http://ecpat.net/EI/Publications/Trafficking/Factsheet_Greece.pdf.

Tainted: *A Lost Innocence* was created by students of the "PhotogenX Around the World Track" (a degree program of University of the Nations* and PhotogenX International). The University of the Nations is a global university with campuses in 142 countries, offering over 600 courses in more than 100 languages. The Track program trains students in photojournalism and Biblical worldview while experiencing the nations of the world firsthand. For more information, visit:

www.taintedinnocence.org

www.photogenx.net

www.avoice4.org

www.uofnkona.edu

*YWAM (Youth With A Mission)
To know God and to make him known

"You may choose to look the other way but you can never say again that you did not know."

— William Wilberforce

ISBN: 978-0-9833952-2-5

Because we care about each of these children,
we have taken measures to ensure their safety
and protect their identities. Certain names
have been changed and some photos are only
representative of their corresponding character,
rather than an actual portrayal.